# Kula Shaker

Publishing Director: **Laura Bamford**

Executive Editor: **Mike Evans**
Editor: **Humaira Husain**

Art Director: **Keith Martin**
Senior Designer: **Geoff Borin**
Design: **Matthew Powell @ Design Revolution, Brighton**

Picture Research: **Maxine McCaghy**

Production Controller: **Dawn Mitchell**

First published in 1997 by
Hamlyn, an imprint of
Reed Consumer Books Limited,
Michelin House, 81 Fulham Road,
London SW3 6RB
and Auckland, Melbourne, Singapore and Toronto

Copyright © 1997 Reed International Books Limited

A Catalogue record for this book is available from the British Library
ISBN 0 600 59270 7

Printed and bound in Great Britain by
Butler & Tanner Ltd, Frome and London

**Picture Acknowledgements**

**Front cover**: Retna/Steve Double
**Back cover**: Retna/Steve Double

**All Action** /David Hardacre 4, /Suzan Moore 39 left, 62, 63, 78/79,
/Ellis O'Brien 80 left
**Alpha** /Richard Chambury 66/67, /Ashley Knotek 34 bottom,
/R.Pelham 10, /Jeff Spicer 13 right, 69, 76/77
**Columbia Records** 74/75
**Corbis-Bettmann** 20 left, /UPI 14 bottom, 57 left
**Famous** /Fred Duval 18/19, 30 left, 49 right, 61 , /Rob Howard 72, 73
**Steve Gillett** 11, 46/47, /Angela Lubrano 23, 43, 56, 60
**Merle Moustafa** 12/13, 49 left, 80 right
**Pictorial Press** 20 right, /J. Cummins/SF 58
**Redferns** /Fin Costello 29 right, /Patrick Ford 24/25, 52/53, 64,
/T.Hanley 33 left, /Mick Hutson 25 right, 42, /Michael Ochs Archives
32 , /David Redfern 33 right, 57 right, /G.Wiltshire 34 top, /Des Willie
54/55, 59
**Retna** /Steve Double 5, 8/9, 8 centre, 30/31, 30 bottom right, 30 top
right, 40, 41 top left, /Ian Tilton 54 left, /Midori Tsukagoshi 28, 29 left
**Rex Features** /Steven Butler 68, /Sutton Hibbert 22, /Roger Sargent
35, /Richard Young 38
**Derek Ridgers** 8 left, 14 top, 16/17, 21, 39 right, 44/45, 51
**S.I.N** /Steve Double 15, 50, 65, /Hayley Madden 26, 41 right, 41
centre left, 70/71, 76 left, /Roy Tee 3, 6/7, /Kim Tonelli 27, 36/37,
/Andy Willsher 48

# Kula Shaker

PAUL LESTER

HAMLYN

# CONTENTS

★★★★★★★★★★★★★★★★

# Early Daze

K ula Shaker, a different kind of Britpop band . . . enter Crispian Mills, the man with the famous thespian background . . . Mills has his mind blown away by rock music generally, and the Kinks in particular . . . then by the Hari Krishna cult . . . and finally by mind-expanding drugs

### RISE AND SHINE

Of all the popular British so-called 'indie' bands that have emerged in the wake of Oasis' extraordinary success – Ash, The Bluetones, Space, Dodgy, Ocean Colour Scene, Cast – unarguably the most outstanding, commercially and artistically, are Kula Shaker.

With their swirling, psychedelic rock, vaguely Buddhist leanings and desire to achieve spiritual freedom by transcending (Western) materialistic notions of worldly happiness, these four young men from South London have managed that rare feat: to capture the (fearful, pre-millenial) mood of the moment as well as the spirit of the times.

In just one year – 1996 – they were chosen as support act by Noel and Liam at their historic Knebworth extravaganzas (even though Kula Shaker are virtually the anti-Oasis, eschewing rock's three Rs – birds, booze and bad behaviour – for their own holy trinity: meditation, metaphysics and mantras); they reached the Top 40 with their first single and the Top 10 with their next three; and their debut album, 'K', knocked The World's Biggest Rock Band, R.E.M., off the Number One slot in the first week of its release.

Not bad for a group who are seen by their detractors as a bunch of middle-class, pseudo-mystical, public school fops obsessed with

**Crispian: Kula geezer**

the past – specifically, that period between 1966 and 1969 when rock began to experiment with new instruments (notably the sitar), new ideas (global harmony, consciousness-raising and peace'n'love), and new drugs (particularly the mind-expanding kind with hallucinogenic properties like LSD). If anything, Kula Shaker have succeeded in spite of, rather than because of, prevailing trends, their wayward, fanciful ideals running counter to the laddish inclinations of many of today's bands.

Kula Shaker's quaintly hippyish fondness for The Beatles at their most far-out (most 90s retro-ists opt for 'Revolver'-era Beatles; Kula prefer 'Magical Mystery Tour'), their tendency towards Eastern philosophy (the Marrakesh, as opposed to Mile End, variety), their journey through the colourful realms of the psychedelic imagination, not forgetting their amockalyptic conviction that The End Of The World Is Nigh – all of these are unusual in themselves.

That Kula Shaker have any strongly-held beliefs at all in these cynical, irony-drenched times is nothing short of remarkable.

## JOURNEY INTO THE PAST

The band actually signed on the dotted line, with Columbia Records, in October 1995. But that wasn't the start of the Kula Shaker story; far from it.

In fact, to find Kula's roots, you would have to go as far back as the mid-80s, to a series of events – some minor, some verging on the cataclysmic – that would eventually lead to the formation of this most unique of modern rock bands.

The background of Kula Shaker's singer, writer, guitarist and all-round visionary-poet-leader, Crispian Mills – Dodge, to his friends — is appropriately unique, too.

Born on January 18th 1973 in Hammersmith, West London, Kula's charismatic, photogenic frontman ('he's got the cherubic looks of a fallen angel,' said one writer, impressed by Mills' Brian Jones-ish blonde mop, sky blue eyes, full, fleshy lips and pale skin) was brought up by his mother, Hayley Mills, a film star in the late 50s/early 60s – her most famous roles were as a pretty little wastrel teenager in *Whistle Down The Wind, Pollyana* and *The Family Way*, the latter also featured a Paul McCartney soundtrack.

Then there was his father, Roy Boulting, a film director who left home when Crispian was just two. Most distinguished of all his relations, however, was his grandfather, John Mills, the highly respected, Oscar-winning, veteran star of many a wartime movie, not to mention scores since. 'My grandad's fucking hard,' eulogised Crispian recently. 'He torpedoed the Nazis.'

This tongue-in-cheek sense of pride towards his grandfather's achievements is fairly indicative of Crispian's desire to play down his illustrious family name, to, as he says, 'lay off the celebrity sibling (sic) angle.' He has always feared that people, and unscrupulous journalists in particular, would use his past as a stick with which to beat him, as an excuse to accuse him of being over-privileged.

'You know what England's like, especially the British press,' he grumbled to the *NME* in an early interview, 'and if that's the whole

Crispian with his famous family: mum Hayley and grandad Sir John

reason you get written about, then what's the point in that, man? If I was a piece of shit and the band was crap and I couldn't play guitar, then talk about that, man. But the band's good, you know?'

The public school-educated Crispian (he went to Stowe School, along with Beatles producer George Martin's son, Giles) did enjoy quite a relaxed upbringing in many ways, but, as he often stresses now, it was not exactly bohemian. 'We weren't like the

Redgraves,' he says, referring to that other famous post-war acting dynasty. 'We never read Marx after dinner.'

It's an upbringing about which he is now learning to be unapologetic. 'It's just my destiny,' he has said. 'I can't really help it.

'Besides, it wasn't, like, massive film premieres and paparazzi following you around all the time.

'Acting,' he explained, 'was just a job, the family business. 'My grandad's an actor, my

TWELVE

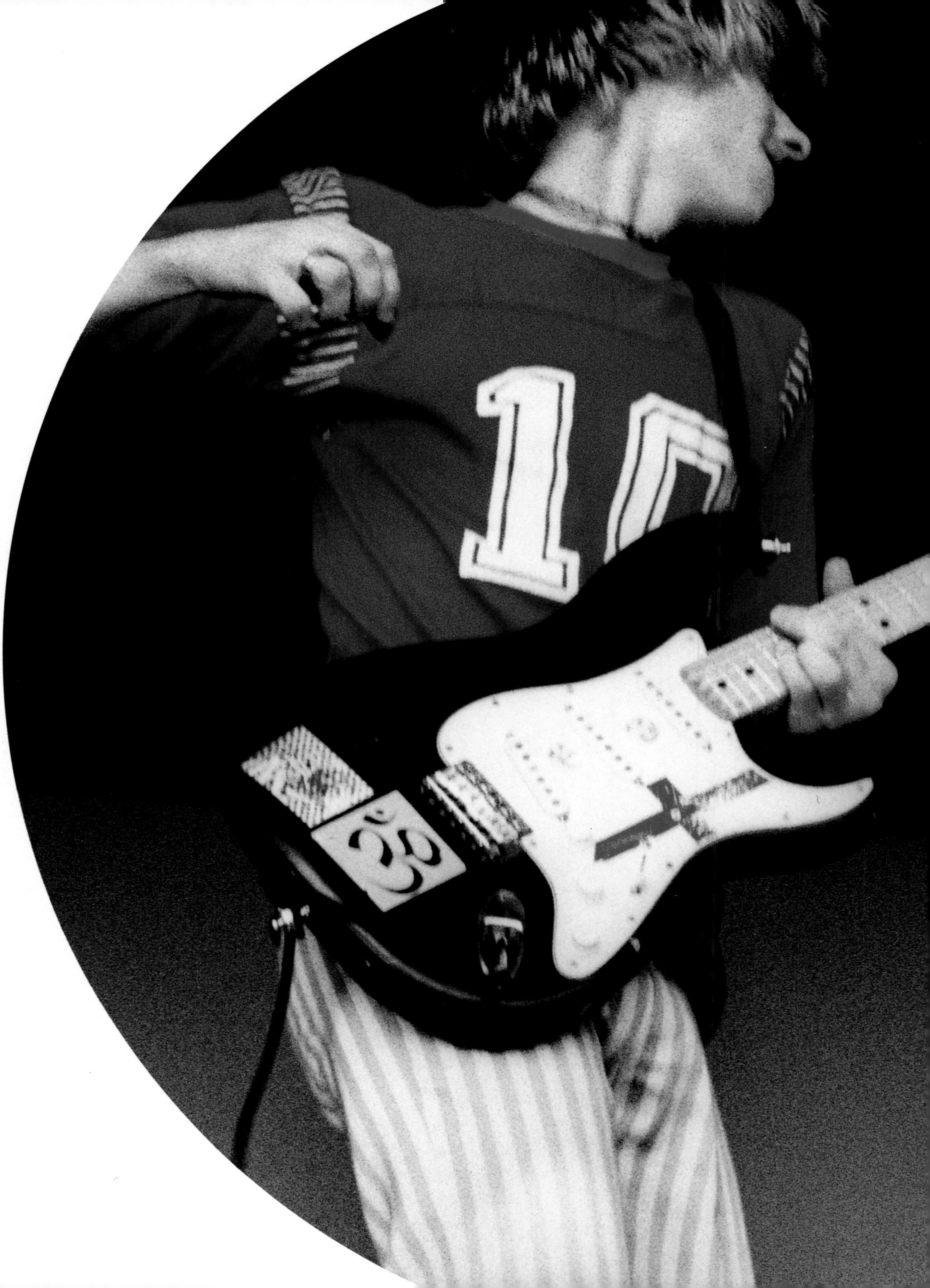

grandmother's a playwright, my mum's an actress, my auntie [Juliet Mills] is an actress, my cousin's a director, my dad was a director and my mum's cousin was an actress. That's just what they did.'

Not that Crispian was ever tempted to follow in his family's footsteps: 'Acting was never an option,' he recalled. 'Too many of my family friends are unemployed. There is very rewarding work in the acting profession, in the theatre, but there's no money.'

The first major thing outside

Crispian had, up to that point, yet to fully grasp the fabulous possibilities of loud guitars and louder drums. That is, until that fateful day when he heard the tinnitus-inducing thump of proto-heavy metal, being played by one of his mother's friends, suddenly come blasting out of one of the rooms at home.

It was The Kinks.

'I'll never forget it,' said Crispian, who had something akin to a quasi-religious experience as he entered the room. 'It was just like walking into a temple. It was the guitar solo on "You Really Got Me" that really made me want to play

Crispian's relatively distinctive family life to have a considerable impact on Mills' teenage brain was his epiphanal initial exposure to the sound and culture of rock music.

the guitar. It was like I'd discovered the holy grail!'

The second crucial event in Crispian Mills' development came shortly afterwards, when his mum, ever open to exotic influences, took him along to the Hare Krishna temple in Letchmore Heath, Hertfordshire (the eerily serene location, incidentally, that inspired John Wyndham's *Day Of The Triffids*), to see the 'weird white guys in robes' and, basically, to soak up some of the karmic atmosphere, man.

'There was a powerful energy there,' recalled the singer, in a voice that has been compared to Mick Jagger's, a slow, measured, cockney-ish drawl that tries in vain to hide its artier pretensions. 'It affected me, because suddenly I started to see that people were into some really weird shit in this world.'

And then, aged 15, came the third Life-Altering Happening. This was when Crispian Mills took his first tab of acid. Mills now admits that he spent the whole of his 'A'

Level years 'tripping off my brain, listening to The Doors.'

But that first night he was no experienced druggy. And so he just lay there, flat on his back, alone in his bedroom, staring up at the photos on his bedroom walls of The Beatles and sundry other 60s cool cats, simultaneously bewitched and bothered by the alternately bland and trashy programmes offered by twilight hour TV, tripping his naive young head off.

When he finally managed to reassemble his post-lysergic scrambled consciousness, Crispian realised that the decade he was fated to grow up in was, in his words, 'depraved and culturally starved.'

As he saw it, it was now down to him, and him alone, to nourish the sick and needy and feed the hungry.

**Wide boy**

**The Doors – a big influence on the teenage Crispian**

# Shine On You Crazy Diamonds

**C**rispian meets Alonza Bevin . . . the pair start up a psychedelic nightclub, the Mantra Shack . . . an early version of Kula Shaker is formed . . . some weirdo 'associates' emerge . . . The Objects Of Desire take shape . . . Mills freaks out, then makes the trip to India . . . and Kula Shaker get their name from an old fakir . . .

### PEOPLE ARE STRANGE

The fourth fateful (or accidental, depending on the extent to which you are seduced by the band's cosmic worldview) step on the road to Kula-dom came with Crispian's encountering, around the late 80s, certain people, some of whom were definitely into 'some weird shit', and all of whom would help direct the young man towards his destiny as focal point of one of the most important new British acts of the late 90s.

In 1988, while he was at Richmond College, Mills met Alonza Bevin, a comparatively normal bloke – that is, if you ignore the vivid dyed-red crop and the description of him by one journalist as 'like a 70s kids TV presenter at one with the dark side.' Mills and Bevin soon discovered that they had a mutual love of all things psychedelic, as well as a keen interest in the legend of King Arthur.

'I've known Crispian since he was knee-high to a grasshopper,' said a candid Bevin. 'When I first met him, though, I thought he was a twat.

'He looked like he was in some kind of timewarp. Cuban heels and dodgy shades,' mocked Alonza, and perhaps rightly so, not least because it was Crispian's insistence on wearing very Cuban-heeled winkle-pickers day in, day out for six years, that means he now suffers from problems with the tendons in his ankles.

That said, the future Kula Shaker bassist did admit that his own predilection for sombre 'goth' outfits was equally ridiculous.

Mills teamed up with Bevin to form a mod-fuelled band, first allegedly called The Lovely Lads, then The New Originals (shades of *Spinal Tap* ??).

By 1990, Crispian was also running a psychedelic nightclub, the Mantra Shack, which was based inside Richmond Ice Rink. It was here that all the local tensomethings hip to the alternative vibe (maaaaaan) would freak out to such hairy crazies as Dr Phibes And The House Of Wax Equations, and flip their collective wig to to the brain-frazzling lightshow, organised by latterday hippy-crusties, Ozric Tentacles.

'The club was really surreal,' Crispian remembers in retrospect, 'because you'd wander out after the full-on lightshow and there would be an ice-rink with an organ playing and everything.'

**Crispian emerges from his timewarp**

Via the band and its attendant 'scene', the pair met Jay Darlington, who Crispian knew because he and Jay once dated two girls who happened to be sisters. Despite this, or maybe not, Darlington was soon invited to join the band as keyboard player.

On a non-musical level, it was Jay's pudding-bowl haircut – trendy at the time because of such Northern 'baggy' outfits as Inspiral Carpets and The Mock Turtles – that Crispian, under the influence of some intoxicant or other, mistook for a German war helmet.

Not that the tonsorial affectations of the also-quite-conventional Darlington put off Crispian Mills and Alonza Bevin from joining forces with him.

'We were in all these dodgy bands, and Jay was hip to the scene,' said Alonza. 'A right groovy little character around town.'

Not everyone thought Crispian and Alonza's early attempts at guitar-heavy rock were 'dodgy'. In fact, many thought they were one of the best live acts they had ever seen. As a consequence, they became the 'house' band, packing out the Mantra Shack on a weekly basis and pulling in as many punters as the more famous likes of Spin (later to become Gene) and Dodgy, who would soon run their own club night there.

Crispian, only in his mid-teens at this point, was something of a prodigy, being incredibly gifted on both the guitar and piano. He could also write impressive songs, even this early on, which is why the majority of the band's set comprised mainly original material, with the odd cover version thrown into the set, such as The Beatles' 'Rain', which Mills particularly favoured for its psychedelic dream-like qualities and reversed-tape guitar track.

Over the next year or so, Crispian, Alonza and Jay would recruit two more members: current Kula Shaker drummer Paul Winter-Hart – another regular-ish geezer – and the rather more eccentric Saul Dismont, who was actually Crispian's cousin. Dismont was the band's vocalist and tambourine man for a while in Kula's pre-history, with Crispian in the role of 'belly-dancing guitarist'.

**The Grateful Dead**

Winter-Hart to finally crystallise the line-up that would become Kula Shaker as we know them today, the original duo of Mills and Bevin were paying their dues by mixing it up with a motley crew of truly bizarre prophets, seers and sages.

Fairly sinister was Don Pecker, a one-time neo-Nazi vegetarian pyromaniac with a fetish for leather who had as much experience behind the wheel (driving taxis) as he (allegedly) had behind bars, and whose presence as the band's 'madness guru' somehow led to their virtually accidental debut festival performance as The Kays, at 1993's Glastonbury festival. About which incident, more later.

Before Pecker, there was the equally strange Marcus Maclaine, the 30-ish lead singer of a South London psychedelic rock troupe called The Objects Of Desire, a band that slowly subsumed The New Originals and which Crispian and Alonza ended up joining for a lot longer than they anticipated – several years, in fact.

While Crispian and Alonza were with The Objects Of Desire, they played the sort of mod-related pop-rock that they're known for

However, Saul, who got a lot of stick in those early days, apparently for his startling physical resemblance to Lenny Kravitz and funky inclinations, was only with the band for a short period – he left to start up that haven for neo-mods, London's Blow-Up club, followed by a stint running an odd little late-night haunt called Magick.

Dismont did stick around just long enough, though, for him to be able to introduce his cousin, Alonza, Jay and Paul to the joys of Eastern mysticism, to the black magic teachings of 19th Century nutter-genius Aleister Crowley, as well as to the magical properties of the letter 'K'.

The latter, seemingly trivial, factor was as significant as anything else in helping shape Kula Shaker's destiny.

## CRAZY DIAMOND GEEZERS

Just as Crispian Mills and Alonza Bevin were joining forces with Jay Darlington and Paul

**Beatles McCartney and Harrison, with Jane Asher and Maharishi Mahesh Yogi**

Alonza, Jay, Paul and Crispian: pavemental!

today, only minus a lot of the mystical references and Eastern ambience. Maclaine was the vocalist, although Mills occasionally sang lead, aided and abetted on harmonies by Darlington and Winter-Hart as and when they were drafted into the group.

While they were together, The Objects Of Desire flitted from name to name like most bands go through groupies, switching with indecent haste between monickers as varied as The Krays, The Trays, The Days and The Gays, before ultimately settling for the aforementioned Kays.

It was only when the band became known as The Kays that Maclaine would finally disappear from the fold. This allowed the current quartet – Mills, Bevin, Darlington and Winter-Hart – to wrest control and steer the group in a new direction.

Maclaine was less than chuffed with being squeezed out of the band. He even sent an angry missive to a music paper recently, accusing Crispian Mills of being a pseudo-mystic and pretending to love music of which he allegedly has little knowledge.

With specific reference to Kula Shaker's debut single, 'Grateful When You're Dead' – whose title was a pun on the legendary 60s acid rockers from America's West Coast, The Grateful Dead – the letter pointed out:

'In the many years that I have known Crispian Mills, he has never shown the slightest interest in Jerry Garcia [head of the Dead]. Indeed, on the rare occasions that the Dead were mentioned, his response tended to be one of scorn or derision.

'They,' the letter ended sarcasticaly 'should re-name themselves Kula Faker.'

It was during Mills' and Bevin's hideously protracted sojourn with Maclaine – the details of which remain cloudy, although one can probably guess at the intensity of the madness that surrounded the band – that, mentally speaking, Crispian went ever so slightly off the rails.

'I turned into a bit of a freak,' as Mills, ever forthright and candid, has put it.

## GO EAST, YOUNG MAN!

To help himself recover from the insanity of the Objects Of Desire phase, Crispian decided to head for India, inspired initially by the spiritual journey Eastwards undertaken by George Harrison during The Beatles' celebrated, exploratory 'Sgt Pepper' phase in the late 60s, when the original Fab Four met the Maharishi Mahesh Yogi.

'Saint George,' Crispian refers to the ex-Beatle and inspirational spiritualist. 'I don't think of him as an old fart with a beard.'

Eager to learn new things and immerse himself in what he saw as a less debauched and depraved culture, Crispian travelled to an off-the-beaten-track village called Mayapoor, deliberately avoiding more trendy locations like, say, Goa, where part-time mystics and fake spiritual zealots have, for many decades, holidayed in other people's misery.

'I stayed well clear of all that raving in dayglo temples crap; fuck that,' said Crispian, in an atypical, momentary lapse of goodwill-to-all-mankindness. 'I'd like to take their tie-dye T- shirts and smelly hair and. . grrr! You know the end of *Apocalypse Now!* when they napalm that beach? I have fantasies about that happening in Goa.'

In Mayapoor, Crispian was looked after and taught by yet another unusual character

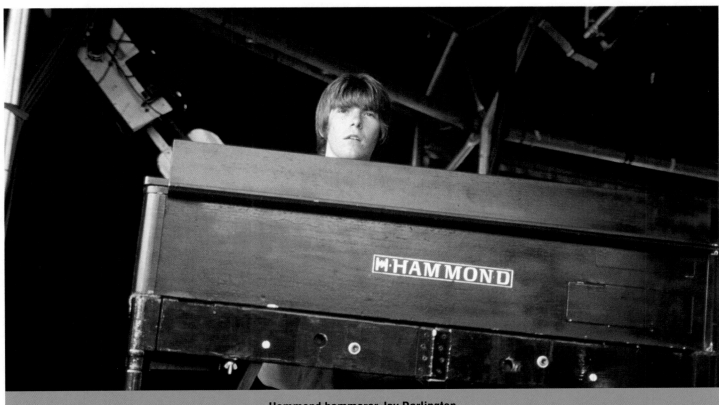

**Hammond hammerer Jay Darlington**

**Kula Shaker some action**

with spiritual inclinations, this one being known as Mathura.

Mathura has been described as a 'monk and revolutionary conspirator', and it was he who gently pushed the open-minded Mills towards a particular brand of Eastern philosophy, named after another mystic called Chaitanya.

Mathura also inspired in Mills a genuine love for Indian music, whose sounds would soon surface in the recordings of Kula

Shaker – although, Crispian is quick to stress, there were elements of Indian music in The Kays (or any other of the pre-Kula variants) before he even set foot in Asia: 'I was already into the vibe,' he insists. 'We just increased it.'

'The reason I went there was to enrich myself,' Crispian explained when he returned from his 10-week journey through India, 'and to experience something that would change my life. It's like going to another planet. You

have to go there and meet the people, get into different philosophies and ways of looking at life.

'India had an enormous effect on me,' he added. 'It's very difficult to explain how I feel, because I don't want to sound pretentious or throwaway. But it was a real spiritual awakening. The people were amazing, and the place was amazing.'

Crispian came home from India a seriously enlightened man, his life finally

given clarity and meaning, his perception of external reality altered forever (and that was without recourse to mind-expanding substances of any kind).

And then it came to pass that the enigmatic Mathura bequeathed the band their new name, albeit indirectly.

This was some time towards the end of 1993, when everyone in the group (except Jay) lived together, *à la* The Monkees or The Beatles in *Help!*, in a house in the posh

North London suburb of Highgate (this followed stints in shared accomodation in Cricklewood – a commune in Child's Hill, to be precise – Swiss Cottage, Finchley Road and an estate in Chiswick).

One day, Mathura turned up with an equally mysterious gentleman called Kula Shakhar in tow.

'He was a very mystical chap,' reminisced Alonza Bevin some time later in an interview conversation with the *Sheffield Electronic Press*, 'although he was actually from around the area we were living in at the time. And he was, in fact, the very first Krishna devotee in Europe.

'Anyway, he was talking about life and the universe and such, and he was talking about his name and his good fortune. He said that the spirit of Kula Shaker – a ninth Century emperor and a very pukka chap, into God and poetry and music – was looking after him, and that, if we took his name, he would watch over us as well.

'And we thought, "Well, we'll have a bit of that, then."'

And so they did.

But not just yet.

**Careful with that axe, Crispian!**

# Hard Daze Knights

**K**ula Shaker: electric warriors . . .
Crispian loves Ritchie Blackmore
. . . meet the other three Kula
boys . . . the studious, handsome
Alonza Bevin . . . the retrospectacular
Jay Darlington, oldest of the bunch . . .
and pig-farming Paul Winter-Hart . . .

## MILLS AND BOONS

Like all great bands, Kula Shaker aren't just one stellar frontman plus a trio of drab, characterless, behind-the-scenes instrumentalists.

Although chisel-cheeked Crispian is the focus, Alonza, Jay and Paul are more than merely proficient sidekicks, adding considerably to the look and overall feel of the group, as well as making crucial creative contributions (they received co-writing credits on most of the 13 tracks on their debut album, 'K').

Kula Shaker as a whole may represent the sum total of their four different experiences and influences, but it's also quite easy to distinguish the four members of the band, to recognise each one's quirks, strangeness and charms.

Living together in those various parts of West and North London in, as they put it, 'the same bubble', may have helped them fuse all the disparate strands of their individual personalities into one distinct reality – the Kula sound/sensibility – and make them work in a highly intuitive fashion.

However, it also highlighted the very real differences between the four players. This was no bad thing, especially when you consider the number of bands who have, since The Beatles and the Stones, disintegrated as a result of warring egos given insufficient space to breathe and room to express themselves.

For sure, Kula Shaker are far more than a vehicle for locquacious ideologue Crispian Mills, whose theatrical background, love of Eastern culture and general air of a dandy beamed down from Carnaby Street circa 1967 have all been well documented – even if his love of early 70s metal monsters, Deep Purple, has been kept quiet.

Indeed, before analysing the individual contributions to Kula Shaker of the other three members of the band, it is worth briefly focusing on this highly illuminating lapse into extreme bad taste of a band whose work has been known at times to teeter precariously on that fine line between the sublime and the naff.

**Ritchie Blackmore**

Because Kula Shaker haven't just been called 'The Stone Roses go to Goa'; they've also been referred to as 'Deep Purple do Delhi'. It's a tag that seems to imply that Kula's music and words amount to no more or less than cod-psychedelic hard rock with an exaggerated love of all things Indian, all of which borders on the burlesque, reducing Kula Shaker to the exploitative level of an 'It Ain't Half Hot, Mum!' for indie kids.

Crispian protests that his fondness for Indian culture is based on a genuine craving to expand the frontiers of his narrow Western mind.

'I found the real value of life in India,' he insists, 'buried deep in my heart, and I have continued to learn it.'

Cynical tactician or not, Mills has extolled the virtues of Purple axeman Ritchie Blackmore on more than one occasion.

'I'm a huge Blackmore fan,' he has revealed. 'He played all that mad, fast lead guitar, but it was really sloppy and had a kind of a garage feel about it. When I first heard "Highway Star" it was like, Wow! Beethoven, man!'

Still. We won't hold it against him.

## THE OTHER THREE

Ignoring such embarrassing admissions as 'Ritchie Blackmore Is God', and leaving aside frontman Crispian Mills for a moment, the first other Kula boy up for close inspection is Alonza Bevin.

A polite, thoughtful, studious man with a distinctly muso bent (he loves his Fender Jazz bass!), this strikingly handsome 26 year-old may smoke roll-ups and may have once been a dustman (true!), but his introspective nature has afforded him the reputation as the conscience of the group.

Bevin's reserved demeanour comes as a surprise when you discover that his mother was once a top model as well as an actress.

Like Crispian, Alonza doesn't like to be pigeonholed as middle class, just because his parents 'had a car, or something. I don't know what the distinctions are for middle class these days, anyway. It means fuck all.'

According to Crispian, Alonza is 'mad on folk', whereas third member, Jay Darlington, the oldest member of the band at 29, is a self-styled 60s disciple.

'I was always called retro at school,' he

**Crispian gets down to it: London's Brixton Academy, January '97**

says, 'but that's what I'm into and if anyone doesn't like it they can sod off. I'm certainly not going to deny it now that it's become fashionable again. Ocean Colour Scene are the most full-on mods around, mind you, far more than we've ever been.'

Darlington has had many jobs in his short life: he was apparently a milkman in Sidcup, a milkman's assistant, a tree feller, a gardener and a fence painter before joining the band in 1994 following stints as vigorous Hammond-hammerer with a variety of obscure local mod outfits.

A droll man whose friendly demeanour can disguise his capacity for witheringly sardonic put-downs, Jay is generally on hand to deflate the more pompous proclamations of Kula's leader, wannabe guru Crispian.

Oddly, Jay was once described by Alonza as 'a sort of mystic man, a celibate monk-like character' and, although Darlington does wear spectacles offstage – lending him a rather more dignified, if not monastic, air – this was probably more a case of the joker being out-joked.

That said, his mother is a spiritualist, the latter occupation the cause of some ribbing in the band.

'He's very much into astral projection,' they have taunted the keyboardist. 'He astrally projects in his sleep. That's why he never does drugs. We don't even let him

have caffeine! He's high on life.'

Perhaps significantly, Darlington was the only member of the band never to live in shared accomodation with the other three, although, as he now admits, he was usually only a few streets away ('I got as close as about 100 yards, which was close enough').

Described by some female Kula devotees as 'cute', due to his blonde hair and angular, male model's face, the 25 year old football fanatic, keen sketcher and painter, Paul Winter-Hart, was born in Somerset and brought up in West Pennard, a stone's

**Seminal influences Frank Zappa and, opposite, Pink Floyd**

One writer has even described Paul as cheekily scatological (ie, obsessed with bodily functions).

'If I could look as half as smart as The Rolling Stones' drummer, Charlie Watts, I'd be very happy,' Paul has said. 'He's splendid looking and he has natural dignity, which is rare for a drummer. I can't do that because I've always got too much spit coming out of my mouth.'

In spite of his BBC newscaster-style pronunciation (his voice has been likened to that of Captain Mark Phillips, the ex-husband of Princess Anne), despite *Smash Hits* having decided that Kula Shaker are 'indie aristocrats', and notwithstanding the fact that the Spice Girls shouted, 'Oi, posho! Get yer tits out!' at Kula Shaker when the two groups met at *Top Of The Pops,* Paul, like Alonza and Jay, actually went to a comprehensive school.

Winter-Hart has actually had quite a lot of experience in the area of 'working class'

throw from Glastonbury, before spending some of his childhood in a 'very haunted house' in Battersea, South London, with his psychic mother.

Like Jay, Paul is prone to onstage bouts of viciousness, and it may come as some surprise to learn that the drummer with the scruffy tendencies has a secret ambition to grow a handlebar moustache – very Edwardian gent (let's face it, he's already got the sideboards).

Paul likes to play the dumb drummer when it suits him; he even interrupted one deep and meaningful bout of soul-searching between the band and a journalist when he burst out with: 'I don't understand why we have to be so heavy. Can we not just talk about hi-hat parts?'

It is a debunking technique that has proved quite handy for Paul, particularly on those frequent occasions when he has needed to escape difficult interview situations, especially those featuring Crispian's more fanciful lexical flights of fancy and grandiose statements re: matters of global socio-political import.

**Page 'n' Plant in full Led Zeppelin glory**

employment: he has been a barman, a double-glazing salesman, a bus driver and – though this is quite possibly a band in-joke – a pig farmer.

'He was rectifying pigs' prolapses,' the others have teasingly insisted, 'and we took pity on him. He seemd like a nice guy. So we got him off the pig farm, brought him back to London from Glastonbury and tried to teach him how to play drums.'

However, Paul does admit that his parents, while not rich, could quite feasibly be described as 'posh'.

That his mother was once a jazz dancer while his mother's first husband played in a jazz band also had a considerable impact on the budding Buddy Rich whose all-time favourite albums are 'Freak Out' by The Mothers Of Invention, the debut LP by Led Zeppelin and Pink Floyd's 'The Piper At The Gates Of Dawn'.

It is the richness of their individual experiences that makes Kula Shaker such an interesting, invigorating propostion.

And it is the truly dazzling diversity of the four Kula boys' musical tastes – from Alonza's folk leanings, to Crispian's beloved classical and Eastern music, to Jay's Beatles, Stones, Who and Small Faces records, to Paul's more idiosyncratic delights – that makes their own recordings so unique and entertainingly eclectic.

**Charlie Watts**

**Paul Winter-Hart takes time off from fiddling with pigs**

# Dark Side Of The Loon

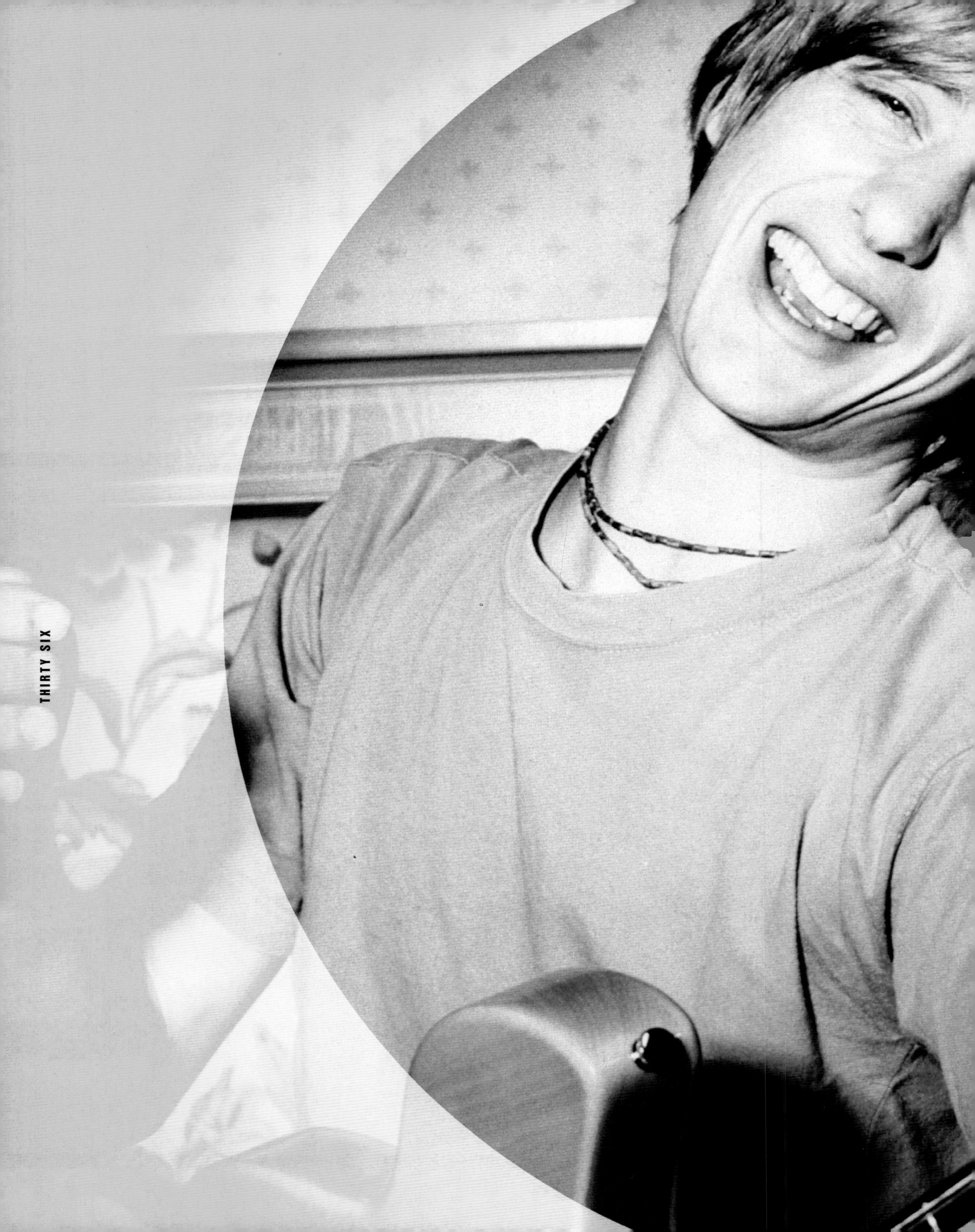

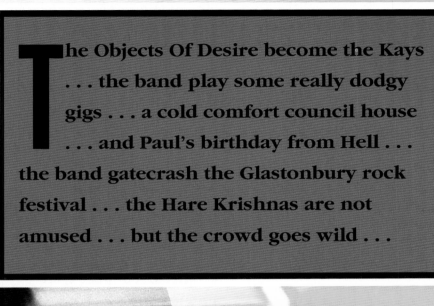

**T**he Objects Of Desire become the Kays . . . the band play some really dodgy gigs . . . a cold comfort council house . . . and Paul's birthday from Hell . . . the band gatecrash the Glastonbury rock festival . . . the Hare Krishnas are not amused . . . but the crowd goes wild . . .

## WEIRD SCENES

Although their rise to prominence may, to outsiders, appear to have been meteoric, in reality during their Kays-to-Kula Shaker transitional phase, the band were going nowhere at the speed of sloth.

Certainly, they haven't always played to thousands of eager Kula kids.

As Paul Winter-Hart says, 'We had plenty of bad gigs, man.'

'We can remember all too clearly all the times when there was no one in the audience,' adds Crispian, wincing at the memory. 'There was one gig at Kentish Town where we put a guitar case on its end and put a coat on top of it and Jay's brother Bill was standing behind it trying to pretend it was a person. Times have been hard.'

Alonza also remembers those pre-success days when the band slogged away in pubs and clubs, 'with nothing going for us, playing solidly for two and a half years until we finally got signed.'

'Gigging, gigging, gigging; crap, crap, crap,' is how Crispian Mills recalls this difficult period of transition when they were still called The Kays (and The Trays and and The Krays and The Gays. . .), a time when the reviews they received in the music press all seemed to say, with damning simplicity: 'The Kays – Wankers.'

The reviewers couldn't have been more wrong; indeed, it would be false to suggest that Kula Shaker only became the great band they are today when they changed their name. Because anybody that attended their early shows as The Kays will tell you that they have always been a good band, that the playing has always been competent and that, if you were a fan back then as well as now, you will have noticed that their music hasn't actually changed that much.

'It was ridiculous that nobody signed them back then,' said a friend from this earlier period. 'They were just as great as they are now.'

Call it fate, call it injustice, call it bad timing – either way, many of the gigs that they played were empty, the band performing in front of the proverbial two men and a bowser.

Then there were the gigs where at least some people actually deigned to turn up, even if most of them weren't exactly there to see the band.

Take, for example, their unforgettable twilight performance at London's trendy niterie, the Leisure Lounge, where the support act was, to say the least, something of a shock . . .

'It was a reverse billing,' says Paul, smiling now, even though, at the time, it was no laughing matter. 'They were on at two in the morning and we were on at four. The act before us, this guy, was swinging weights and irons and swords from his dick and his nipples and stuff like that. By the time we came on, it was 4.30 and we were expected to play in this enormous club in front of 50 people coming down from smack.

'And he was playing really loud techno,' emphasises Crispian.

'And his naked girlfriend was smoking crack onstage.'

'And there were loads of drunken goths on speed,' chips in Alonza, piling on the miserable memories.

'It wasn't,' Paul comically understates, 'a particularly happy experience.'

### THE ONLY WAY IS. . . UP?
In fact, the Leisure Lounge nightmare wasn't simply a low point for the band; it also

turned out to be a real turning point in their development.

Quite simply, things couldn't get much worse for them.

Because they had less and less money as time went on, so their standard of living began to get worse and worse and their shared flats, houses and communes became increasingly dilapidated.

In addition to this, even though they managed to get a record contract-cum-development deal with plugging company Gut Reaction, (home of Scally band, Space, and dome-headed popsters, Right Said Fred) this, too, came to nothing and, before long, the band and the label parted company.

'They were always great live,' says Graham Beattie, formerly an A&R man at Gut Reaction who, to this day, can't fathom out why it took so long for the band to make it.

Beattie goes on to explain that the demo tapes that the band worked on during this period – produced by none other than Giles Martin, Crispian's school pal and offspring of silver-haired Beatles knob-twiddler, George – were raw, yet oozed potential.

Ironically, as Beattie also points out, many of Kula Shaker's future classics had already been written and recorded by this time.

'They hadn't written "Tattva" yet, but "Govinda", in particular, was really popular in the office where I worked.'

And yet, 'Govinda' or no 'Govinda', the band were still in the financial, commercial and spiritual doldrums.

Matters seemed to reach crisis point one particularly dreadful night when the council house that Paul, Alonza and Crispian were sharing became so cold that Mills' girlfriend was forced to move out.

Winter-Hart recalls that fateful night – it was also his birthday, poignantly – only too well.

There were the cerebellum-frazzling trips resulting from too many dodgy magic mushrooms, the sub-zero-temperature rooms with ice on the walls, the disturbing noises emanating from the stereo, not to mention the hordes of people who had, probably with the best of intentions, descended on the house to help the poor sod celebrate the worst birthday of his life.

And then, as if to really rub salt in his wounds, Reef – the British rock band who enjoy tremendous success in America, and the group with whom The Kays would tour extensively after their dramatic name change – turned up.

'There I was, tripping off my head, there were loads of people all over the place – I was in a really bad way,' Paul zeroes in on that awful night with painful precision. 'And there were Reef, travelling the world while we were stuck in this freezing council house without a record deal.'

## GLASTER BLASTER

Far less soul-destroying, though no less fraught with incident, was The Kays' debut festival appearance, down at Glastonbury in summer 1993.

Enter Don Pecker, the gonzoid 'madness guru' from Chapter Two and former close friend of 60s teenybop icon turned avant-garde balladeer, (the one-time main man of the Walker Brothers) Scott Walker.

As Crispian explains, Pecker exerted a profound influence on the band in their formative days.

'People like Don helped shape the identity of the band,' he says of the man who emerged from his stint in prison with strange powers and decidedly weird visions.

Basically, as far as Kula Shaker are concerned, it's usually been a case of: watch out, Pecker's about. . .

'One day,' recounts Crispian, 'Don and his wife were sitting round watching TV on lygactol, the sedative. And this girl was looking at Don, eyeing him up and sticking her tongue out, and he suddenly felt really tired, and he became paralysed.

'As this happened, he could feel her coming out of her body like an astral projection. And then he realised that she was in his body and his whole being had this incredible orgasm.'

Far out.

Crispian first encountered Pecker in a Krishna temple earlier that same year. Several months later, The Kays found themselves, acid-fried but excited, travelling down to Glastonbury in a battered Mercedes with this unsavoury character straight out of an old Hammer horror film.

Unfortunately, the car had been reported stolen, and so it was that the hapless Crispian and the sinister Mr Pecker found

themselves banged up at Her Majesty's Convenience. Mercifully, the Somerset police force soon saw sense and, realising they had arrested the wrong people, released them just in time for Pecker and Mills to re-join Alonza, Paul and Jay outside Glastonbury's Krishna tent.

And then something even more bizarre happened: the magical combination of LSD-fuelled confidence and 'I-fought-the-law-and-the-law-lost' bravado conspired to inspire The Kays to perform a whole set's worth of Eastern-tinged psychedelic rock before the entire field full of bemused festival revellers who didn't really know the band from Adam. Crispian claims he will never forget that totally mad afternoon.

'We put up our own 10-man army tent, stole some power off the Hare Krishnas and started playing Indian mantra jams,' he remembers vividly. 'The band was totally straight, but the audience were all tripping on acid, and for an hour we were just dreadful. And then we just got on it. Suddenly, there were 200 hippies dancing to us! The Krishnas weren't too pleased, though.'

Apparently, the aforementioned religious sect weren't happy, and certainly not at all prepared, for the maximum heaviosity of The Kays' overburdened, overwhelming and totally strange drum-heavy sound.

'We weren't actually going down that well until we started improvising "Govinda" on the spot,' says Paul, picking up the story from Crispian. 'Now, I've played gigs with seven or eight other bands in my time, but I've never, EVER seen so many people lock their eyes onto someone like they did with Crispian at that point. Twenty, then 50, then 200 people in this tent with all their eyes locked on Crispian.

And I just thought, "Fuck. . ."'

**Some hippies at Glastonbury prepare to be dazzled by Kula Shaker**

# Time Of The Signs

### IN THE CITY

And then, as if by Far Eastern magic, they became Kula Shaker.

Suddenly, almost overnight, everything was OK in Kula land and things started happening fast for the band.

'The change of name drew a line over our previous work,' says Crispian.

And it was all thanks to the letter 'K'.

'They always set a lot of stall by "K" words,' says Graham Beattie, who now works as A&R man for Radar Records. 'After that name change, it went mad for them.'

Beattie was up in Manchester in September 1995 for the annual In The City new band contest, when he saw Kula Shaker perform before an enraptured crowd which included music business moguls and hardcore indie devotees.

'They were brilliant,' says Beattie of Kula

**The Kays become Kula Shaker . . . the band win Manchester's annual In The City new band competition . . . the hardest gigging band in showbusiness go on the road with The Presidents Of The United States of America . . . the writing's on the wall, they sign to Sony on St George's Day**

Shaker. 'They've always been great at getting crowds going.'

Beattie has never seen Kula Shaker as a flash-in-the-pan, gimmick-laden band, either, notwithstanding their conspiracy theories, visions of Armageddon and the liberal use of Sanskrit in their lyrics. Indeed, he predicted long term success for the band as far back as their days with Gut Reaction.

'It couldn't happen to a nicer bunch of guys,' he says of their current success and popularity. 'They deserve all the success that's coming to them.'

In fact, everybody in Manchester was impressed by Kula Shaker's live prowess, as well as by their experimental songs that managed to combine Eastern influences with poppy accessibility, their dance-tinged beats neatly underpinning the somewhat 60s feel of the melodies.

In the end, the In The City judging panel, blown away by Kula Shaker yet faced with an excellent clutch of exciting new bands, awarded joint first prize to Kula Shaker, Placebo and Performance.

The policy of Kula Shaker's manager Kevin Nixon – formerly the brains behind poodle-haired metal merchants, Little Angels – of making sure the band toured hard whenever possible, had clearly paid off.

Around this time, Kula Shaker went on the road as support band to Corduroy (formerly known as mod revivalists, Boys Wonder), Killjoy, surf-grungers Reef (for whose partisan audience Crispian had to come onstage on rollerblades, to appease the skateboarding punks), as well as US goofball rockers The Presidents Of The United States Of America.

The latter band – 'great ambassadors for entertainment,' according to Paul, his tongue actually nowhere near his cheek – attracted a particularly up type of crowd, which would, in turn, rub off on to the American band themselves, who would run into Kula Shaker's dressing room after Kula's finished set, beaming, 'Oh, dude! That was so joyous! So spiritual!'

It was during their time on the road with The Presidents that Kula Shaker finally realised the importance of not taking themselves too seriously.

Many critics of the band have failed to grasp the irony inherent in their punning songtitles ('Hey Dude', 'Grateful When You're Dead', 'Knight On The Town'), and the humour which they generally try to bring to proceedings as a way of tempering the often po-faced nature of their lyrical concerns.

'We're not exactly a comedy band like the Presidents,' said Paul Winter-Hart, 'but I hope we don't take ourselves too seriously. Some of the things Crispian comes out with,

**Fender bender!**

**Mr Charisma**

we can't just hear them and keep a straight face. He even takes the piss out of himself afterwards!'

Certainly, humour has played an underacknowledged role in the band's success, both in their music, and in the way they approach being in a band. It helps them cope with the stresses and pressures of being one of the hardest working bands in the business.

Not that their astonishing work rate – over 200 gigs in one year alone – has gone at all unrecognised.

'They have succeeded by doing things in a traditional rock'n'roll way: by sheer hard work, by having a ton of good songs, by playing damn well and, in Crispian Mills, having a very charismatic front person,' the group's publisher, Dave Massey, explained to *Music Week*.

Added Massey: 'When you leave a Kula Shaker gig, you feel elated and exhilarated. And you see all sorts of people in their crowds, from teenagers up to fortysomethings – that should tell you why they're successful.'

## ZEN AND THE ART OF LUNAR CYCLE MAINTENANCE

The next step towards infiltrating the mainstream with their exotic-pop music came when, three months after transforming, subtley though crucially, from The Kays to Kula Shaker, and only one week after their In The City triumph, the band signed to Columbia Records.

'Three weeks after changing our name, RCA were the first to offer us a deal,' recalls Alonza, referring to the company who paid for the band to record some new demos – demos that were, according to everyone who has heard them, a vast improvement on the tapes of their early recordings. 'And then it seemed like everybody wanted to offer us deals. So it obviously worked for us.'

Immediately, there was the inevitable record company scramble to sign Kula Shaker once each company knew all the others were keen (like the stock exchange and futures market, the rock industry is all about 'perceived interest'). And yet, no matter how extravagant and generous the amounts of money dangled before their eyes, the band insisted on signing with Columbia, a subsidiary of the giant Sony corporation.

Why? Because they would be the only young rock band on the label's roster, thus affording them priority treatment ('I wanted the band to have their own space,' says manager Kevin Nixon).

Also, because of the strength of Sony's alternative sales force, the band believed the company could break them on the indie circuit first, and the mainstream second, thus affording them credibility as well as commercial potential.

Oh, and of course, because the increasingly superstitious, and astrologically inclined foursome were fatally attracted to the numbers displayed on the wall outside the multi-national conglomerate's Central London offices.

'The most lucky combination of numbers for us is two 10s together and right outside their building it just said 10 10, and we just said, "That's a sign," and went for it,' explains Crispian.

Mills also explains why the band chose to sign the deal at such a specific time that it was actually dependent on the arrangement of the planets.

**The hardest-working guitarist in showbiz**

**Destiny brought them together**

'We consulted our Vedic astrologer, and he recommended a certain lucky moment.'

Not surprisingly, this startling piece of cosmological decision-making was the cause of some near-hysterical scenes down at the Sony HQ.

'The people at Sony were running around, going, "Quick, quick, we've only got five minutes and Jupiter isn't in conjunction with Mercury any more."'

Ronnie Gurr, currently creative director at V2 Records, but back then A&R manager at Columbia and also the man who picked up the Kula baton from talent scout Miles Kemp, told Andrew Male of *Select* magazine that it was the quickest deal Columbia had ever turned round. It was infact completed in 12 working days, although he had personally been on the band's trail for months before that.

However, Gurr did admit that 'the mystic thing nearly blew the deal.' According to Kula Shaker's demands, the contract had to be signed at precisely 10.10pm on St George's Day, with the moon in its fourth quarter. Why St George's Day? Because, as Crispian explains, 'it's a very significant day to Rosicrucian alchemists. It wasn't deliberate. It was destiny.'

Ah. That clears that up, then.

★★★★★★☆★☆★☆★★★★★

# Single Daze

**T**op producer John Leckie to work with Kula . . . 'Grateful When You're Dead' is the band's first single release . . . Noel Gallagher plugs the band . . . 'Tattva' storms the charts . . . 'Hey Dude' almost reaches Number One . . . 'Govinda' brings a taste of India to *Top Of The Pops* . . .

## LECKIE GUYS

As soon as Kula Shaker signed to Columbia, the company immediately put the band in a studio with the knob-twiddler *du jour,* John Leckie. Leckie was intially attracted to the band's sound ('the heavy, psychedelic pop, the mad, jazzy drums, the classic Hammond organ sound and Crispian's guitar work,' as he himself put it), while Kula themselves were intrigued by the experienced rock journeyman with the wild, silver, sorceror's hair.

**The Stone Roses**

John Leckie is a highly acclaimed producer in his forties who has worked with some of the most influential names in rock history: Paul McCartney, John Lennon, George Harrison, Pink Floyd, Magazine, The Fall and Simple Minds. He has also been a major force behind the recent success of Cast, Elastica and Radiohead.

Of all Leckie's impressive credits, however, the adult Crispian Mills was most taken with a rhythmically propulsive chunk of club-influenced indie-dance featuring some incredible funky drumming that he heard, some years before, at the height of the 'Madchester' era in autumn 1989.

The band was The Stone Roses and the track in question was 'Fools Gold' – at that time, the mercurial Manchester outfit's

biggest hit to date. This meant that they would be making their debut appearance on *Top Of The Pops.*

It was a historic episode of the programme, as it turned out, because both key 'Madchester' acts were on that night – the Happy Mondays had also charted the same week with the brilliant 'Rave On' EP. Many of today's top bands, from Cast to Oasis to The Bluetones, now cite this one *Top Of The Pops* episode as being a key event in their development.

Also sitting transfixed in front of his TV that night was the young Crispian Mills.

'I know this sounds really crap, but "Fools Gold" really affected me,' Crispian spoke to *Vox* magazine about the track that would exert such an influence on Kula Shaker, and whose echoes could be heard a while later, on their own hits, 'Grateful When You're Dead' and 'Hey Dude'.

'When it came out it was like a major track. Bad indie bands couldn't get that kind of groove together and I was just really happy because they were using wah-wah.

'I was about 14 and I'd been listening to "Shaft" [the funk soundtrack to the blaxploitation film of the same name, which came courtesy of wah-wah godfather, Isaac Hayes] and "White Room" by Cream. It was such a massive deal hearing a modern band using wah-wah and being cool.'

Jay Darlington is quick to join in with his bandmate's heartfelt eulogy of the Roses when he states, in no uncertain terms: 'They made guitars cool again after all that synth shite in the 80s.'

Leckie it was, then.

## DEAD DEAD GOOD

Kula Shaker's first single proper (Columbia issued a 2,000 limited-edition seven-inch version of 'Tattva', also known as 'Kula 1', in late 1995) was 'Grateful When You're Dead', released in April 1996.

Opening with a deep guitar riff, pounding bass notes and wild wah-wah, the song pursues a Jimi Hendrix-ian melody (circa 'If Six Was Nine') with Led Zeppelin-ish fervour while the 'ba, ba, ba's' of the chorus recall

the 'Pearl & Dean' theme beloved of cinema advertisers in the 70s (the latter, coincidentally, was turned into a hit by the group Goldbug, one month before Kula's own debut single charted).

With its punning title, 'Grateful When You're Dead' paid homage to Jerry Garcia, the late, great, visionary leader of the legendary Grateful Dead who was the focus of much of the world media's attention during the First Summer Of Love – based around San Francisco in 1967 – and who sadly died in 1995.

Lyrically, it posits the idea of the literally dead Deadhead, up in the clouds, playing with the gods, waiting for Kula's arrival ('We're going to have a jam with Jerry Garcia!' a mischievous Crispian told *Sky Magazine).*

It has also been suggested that the song is about the inevitable loss of ego that occurs after death, and the orgasmic pleasure that one (apparently) feels in the afterlife, on having ascended to heaven.

On another level, it took a humorous sideways glance at the sort of blissed-out acid casualties who continued to frequent The Grateful Dead's enormodome gatherings well into the 90s, well up, in fact, until the untimely demise of Jerry Garcia; the sort of 'individualists' who end up conforming to 'alternative' lifestyles; the sort of suggestible loonies who saw God in every Garcia utterance (the sort, indeed, who probably read too much into Crispian Mills' own Anglo-Sanskrit mantrafests).

'Something happens at Grateful Dead concerts,' Crispian told *iD* magazine. 'It's like they get zapped with the Deadhead laser, you know? One second it's, like, "Hey, let's check the gig out," and then, when the band start up – zoiiing! – "Maaan, Jerry's jammin' so haaard!!"'

The extra 'track' on the end of 'Grateful When You're Dead' is a real rambling exercise in stoner prog-rock studio noodling. Featuring heartbeat tom-toms, a pseudo-mournful guitar figure and Jay Darlington's Doors-esque organ washes, it is called 'Jerry Was There'.

The track's endlessly repeated title, courtesy of Crispian doing his best Jim Morrison-as-possessed-preacherman impression, provides another laconic look at those Garcia obsessives who, even as this is being written, are probably soaking up the poor devil's vibes around his grave.

'"Grateful When You're Dead" was originally intended as a bit of a piss-take,' Crispian confirmed in *Vox*. 'But when he died we added the "Jerry Was There" coda. We kind of knew that all these Deadheads would be wandering around going, "Wow, can you feel it? Jerry's here, man!"'

'Grateful When You're Dead', then, lampooned both the 60s hippies and the slacker kids of the 90s; it was a wry critique of two generations of zonked-out headcases.

And yet this was no supercilious put-down on the part of Mills and Co, not when you considered their own trippy gear, Brian Jones haircuts, patchouli image and highly esoteric worldview, as well as their deep affection for rock music at its most fantastical and transcendental.

As such, 'Grateful. . .' served to emphasise that Kula Shaker were rather more prepared to laugh at themselves than their critics would ever have guessed.

The B-side, 'Under The Hammer', ostensibly written about the band's demoralising pre-Kula days, was something else entirely, an explosion of guitars and noise that inspired some of the most unhinged rock journalism in recent memory when it was reviewed in *Melody Maker*.

'Strange, mystical vocals blend into soaring, hallucinatory sequences and gravity-defying rock squizzles, in a molten, impressionistic hurricane of sound just pinned to the firmament by a direct, frizzling pop/rock song,' raved the writer, before thudding back to earth with the relatively mundane observation: 'They're like The Stones Roses if they went to Goa – with John Squire still on guitar, of course.'

'Grateful When You're Dead' entered the charts at Number 35 in April, thanks in part to the patronage of several key players in the music industry. First and foremost was Radio 1FM's Chris Evans, who played the single to death on his breakfast show.

Then there was Noel Gallagher, who surprised everyone by turning up in his chauffeur-driven Rolls Royce at Kula Shaker's 100 Club gig in early '96 and was soon describing them on Steve Lamacq and Jo Whiley's 1FM *Evening Session* as 'the best band in Britain'. This in turn prompted a major article in London's *Evening Standard*, the heading on the front page of the newspaper, next to a photo of Kula Shaker,

**A member of the crowd goes wild!**

reading – surprise! – 'Oasis Say This Is The Best Band In Britain.'

The success of 'Grateful. . .' was also due in part to the special late-night session recorded by the band for 1FM DJ Mark Radcliffe's programme, as well as to the band's two crucial TV appearances: the first on *Top Of The Pops* and the second on Channel Four's *The White Room,* the latter also hosted by Radcliffe.

To some outsiders, the emergence of these four handsome dudes who could play their respective instruments superbly and made an accomplished psychedelicised noise, smacked of record company contrivance. Some cynics believed the band were co-conspirators in an attempt to sell a manufactured act to a gullible public keen to swallow the next big thing after Britpop – Trip pop. However, to anyone who had been following the Kula Shaker story with interest knew that their debut entry was both long overdue, and highly deserved.

As Jo Cavanagh, product manager at Columbia, has rightly observed: 'A lot of people thought they had sprung from nowhere.' Of course, nothing could be further from the truth: Kula's loyal fanbase took ages to build. And this was no assembly-line rock band, either – Kula Shaker had lived and breathed the music they made for years.

**Jerry Garcia**

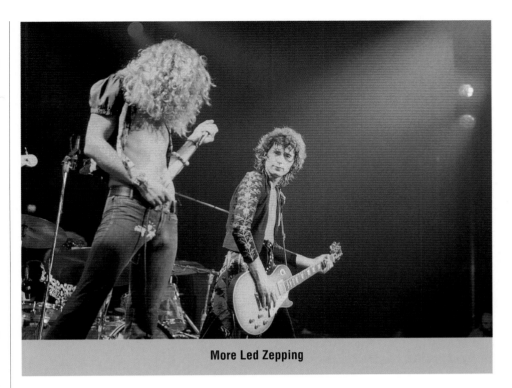

**More Led Zepping**

### TATTVA-VA-VA-VOOM!

Kula Shaker's second single was 'Tattva', the one that really catapulted them into the mainstream and brought their alien sound into thousands of homes, almost like an *X Files* for the ears.

Released in July, 'Tattva' was either a beautifully constructed, perfectly polished slice of Eastern-influenced guitar pop, or a karaoke version of psychedelic-era Beatles, depending on whether you were a fan of the band, or one of their many detractors, the latter increasing in number in direct proportion to Kula's rapidly escalating sales.

Against a delicate sitar pattern, a multitracked choir of Crispians sang heavenly harmonies as the mantra which gave the single its title was repeated by Mills as if in a tranced-out state.

This outrageously infectious, psychedelic singalong made it seem, for a few glorious weeks, as though we had all been beamed back from summer 1996 to summer 1969. Unsurprisingly, it skyrocketed to Number Four in the charts within the first week of its release.

The title, 'Tattva', was taken from a 500-year-old Indian dictum which means, 'The inconceivable simultaneous oneness and difference of reality.' It was apparently written by a saint called Chaitanya (see Chapter Two), and it supposedly contains the secrets of the universe.

Instant karma. Just like that.

Sung in the original Sanskrit – 'the language of the Gods,' according to Mills – the main part of the lyric goes: 'Acintya, bheda bheda Tattva'.

Crispian mysteriously heard the saying twice in the same week, from two completely different people.

'That really blew me away. I told a psychologist what it meant, and he said that, when it is universally understood, we would have the next leap in consciousness, because it basically means that we're all one, all made of the same stuff. Religion, racism – all spiritual problems could be solved.

'It's about the relationship between God and the living entity,' he expanded.

'Imagine the full-blown explanation of the meaning of everything, a condensed kernel of knowledge that you can write books this thick on,' Crispian demonstrated with his fingers, then teetering on the edge of preciousness when he added:

'It's very ancient and is spoken only by very special people.

**Jimi Hendrix**

'The thing about the song is that it's been infused with healing power and magic,' he said as 'Tattva' glided with indecent ease straight into the Top Five. 'That's why it's been so successful.'

He also considered it a subversive presence in the Top 40, 'subverting the system through the system' with its peaceful yet defiant call to alms. Crispian even appeared on an MTV programme and naughtily condoned the use of psychedelic drugs on a live phone-in.

'Tattva' was awarded Single Of The Week in *NME*, the writer extolling its virtues thus: '"Tattva" boasts a glorious tune reminiscent of the Roses, all the cocky bravado of the Gallaghers, Paul Weller's smart grace and a hint of classic Smiths. "Tattva" is where Kula's evolution becomes a revolution.'"

The extra tracks, unavailable elsewhere, that came with the various versions of 'Tattva', were the lilting, sitar-led 'Dance In Your Shadow', which was rather reminiscent of The Beatles' 'You've Got To Hide Your Love Away', or even Oasis' 'Wonderwall'; 'Moonshine', with its delicate Oriental rhythms and spectral keyboard sounds; and the semi-acoustic, somewhat folk-ish 'Red

Balloon', which vaguely recalled 'the British Bob Dylan' – that mid-60s flower power guru, Donovan.

Notwithstanding all the feelings of positivity that it encouraged, the success of 'Tattva' did, however, have one negative outcome. This was the snide accusations of retro-mongering which continued to be hurled at the group.

Not that Crispian agreed with any of them.

'I don't agree with the people who say we make retro music,' he said attacking his critics. 'We're not in any patchouli-soaked pigeonhole. "Tattva" may hark back to the 60s – by all means, I'll let them have that one – but having heard "Govinda", having heard "Hey Dude", it's like, Fuck off! They've got elements that nobody has ever heard before; I've certainly never heard anything like "Tattva" before.

'Besides,' he added, not to be outwitted, 'it's not about us wanting to sound like The Small Faces or whoever, it's about that spirit, attitude and idealism being relevant now as a means to progress forward.'

As long as they distanced themselves from the dreaded 80s ('Basically, there were drum machines and lots of hairspray, and, er, that's it,' they summed up the previous decade in one pithy sentence), and as long as no one tried to dump them in the Britpop category, Crispian didn't really care that much. 'Most of that stuff is so shallow,' he said of his peers. 'Blur, Britpop, flip flop, plip plop – our generation have just got their minds turned off.' He added 'Pulp are really good, really funny, but there's a lot of mediocre crap around.'

Techno innovator and all-round musical futurist, Liam Howlett of The Prodigy, really helped ultimately banish any notions of retro-activity when, after being seduced by the mesmeric properties of 'Tattva', he invited Crispian to record a track with him, one that Crispian later described as 'the mother of all mantras.'

By the summer, the whole of Britain had succumbed to 'Tattva' fever.

'I turned on the TV one day and it was playing in the hairdressers on *Coronation*

*Street,* man,' Crispian told the *NME*. 'It's fucking unreal. All I know is that in six months' time, there's gonna be some knock-on effect from all this. Like what? Some mass elevation of consciousness, definitely.'

## DUDE AWAKENING

Single number three was 'Hey Dude', a ferociously fast and funky blast of storming drumming and freaky wah-wah pedalling that harked back to every gloriously explosive guitar-centric track in history, from Hendrix to The Isley Brothers to the Roses' 'Fools Gold', yet somehow managed to outdo all of its forebears as soon as it reached its 'Hey, dude, don't lean on me, man' chorus.

According to Crispian, the title of 'Hey Dude', a pun on The Beatles' 'Hey Jude', belied its actual message, which was fairly evident as soon as you clapped awestruck ears on the 'All I have is all I need but not enough for greed' anti-materialist lyric. 'It's more than just a piss-take of that deadly serious reverence of The Beatles that's going on at the moment,' explained the singer.

Instead, Mills expanded, it was about being 'a slug when you could be an angel,' a song directed at people who aim too low *vis-à-vis* personal contentment and spiritual fulfillment; the type of people who crave transient earthly pleasures like sex and drugs when they should be pursuing more noble, long-lasting objectives. 'I'm not in a band just because I'm after the next line of coke or to fuck some groupies or shit,' said Crispian, almost setting himself up as some kind of New Puritan (although the subtext of the line, 'You treat me like a woman when I feel like a man' again seemed to scream 'PLEASE DON'T TAKE US TOO SERIOUSLY!')

'Hey Dude' entered the charts at Number Two and its different versions (there were at least two available, both in lavishly packaged CD sleeves, complete with posters and lyrics) came with several extra tracks.

CD1 contained the rambling 'Troubled Mind', which started off gently enough, then built towards a climactic orchestra of guitars and keyboards, before trailing off gently again; an alternate version of 'Grateful When

You're Dead' taken from Mark Radcliffe's radio show; and a new song called 'Into The Deep', also recorded live at 1FM, another mid-paced slice of mod-ish psychedelia.

Meanwhile, CD2 contained a version of 'Tattva' live on Radcliffe, plus 'Drop In The Sea' (a wistful little acoustic, folk-ish number about how wisdom can set people free) as well as something called 'Crispian Reading From The Mahabharata'.

The Mahabharata was one of the two main Indian epics – a story about the war between the Kauravas and the Pandavas and has been described by Crispian as 'an advanced version of the Knights Of The Round Table' – and featured Mills, against a barely audible 'Tattva' backdrop, reciting various extracts from the ancient tale.

It was like *Jackanory* on acid.

## GO, 'VINDA, GO!

KULA Shaker's fourth single, and their third Top 10 entry (it reached Number Seven), of 1996 was 'Govinda'. It was probably the furthest Kula Shaker had gone yet in embracing Indian culture and assimilating the music of the East in their own records.

Basically, there wasn't a single word of English on it!

The title apparently translated as some kind of request for eternal love and beauty in an unkind world.

'It's about attempting to bring Eastern spirituality to the West,' pontificated Crispian Mills on Radio 1FM's news and information programme, *The Net,* adding:

'All true music is spiritual, but it's difficult, in the 20th Century, to achieve music of that type in the West.'

'It's a mantra that's been around for thousands and thousands of years,' added bassist Alonza Bevin. 'We just sort of put it to a pop tune.'

Clarified Crispian: 'It's one of the names of Krishna. Actually, it's also a prayer to try and bring Heaven back down to Earth.'

Extra cuts on the various versions of the 'Govinda' single included several remixes of the title song, one of which, by trendy dance outfit, Monkey Mafia, received a glowing review in club bible *DJ Magazine*, praising its 'slow and gentle dubbed beat.'

In addition, there was a live recording of their single 'Hey Dude' from a concert the band had performed at London's Astoria earlier in the year, as well as another track called 'The Leek'.

'The Leek' was interesting if only because it shed yet more light on Kula Shaker's underacknowledged mischievousness: it was a recording of Alonza Bevin on Andrew Collins and Stuart Maconie's Radio 1FM evening show, answering questions, in *Mastermind*-style, on what was apparently Bevin's 'specialist subject' – the Welsh vegetable of the title!

Finally, there was another new track called 'Gokula', which became the cause of a certain amount of controversy just before 'Govinda' was released.

The naggingly familar guitar riff on 'Gokula' was instantly memorable for very good reason: although it sounded just like Lenny Kravitz's 'Are You Gonna Go My Way' hit from several years back, it appeared for the first time in 1968, on 'Wonderwall', the debut solo LP by George Harrison (this was actually the first solo album by any of The Beatles), on a track called 'Skiing'.

In fact, Kula Shaker made history with 'Gokula'. When word got out that the band were to use the aforementioned guitar riff, The Beatles' publishers, Northern Songs, put a spoke in the works with their blanket ban on all Beatles material being used for anything other than cover versions – no samples, no musical quotations, nothing.

However, the indomitable Kula Shaker were not to be defeated.

Crispian Mills sent a personal letter to George Harrison, asking if the band could use the track, and Harrison did, indeed, convey his permission to Northern Songs. Thus, 'Gokula' was the first ever Beatles-related song to be used in this way.

Perhaps this explains why another of the remixed versions of 'Govinda' that appeared on the CD single was titled 'the St George mix' – as a way of thanking the great man.

**Kula meditate on the meaning of life**

★★★★★★ ★★★★★★★★

# Top Of The Poppadoms

## OH, 'K'!

'K', Kula Shaker's debut album, was released in September 1996, and an intriguing proposition it was, too.

Before you even got to the music, there was plenty to occupy the listener. Like the packaging and artwork, which recalled nothing so much as the collage Peter Blake had created for The Beatles' great 'Sgt Pepper' masterpiece.

The artwork for 'K' – indisputably one of the first major concept albums of the 90s – once again emphasised Kula Shaker's endless commitment to the 11th letter of the alphabet.

Because there, on the front cover, was a painting, which originally sprang from Crispian Mills' ever-fertile imagination (he had doodled it on a bit of paper!), but which was actually drawn and inked by Dave Gibbons, one of the original illustrators of the cult favourite *2000AD* comic.

The painting featured a giant Krishna surrounded by 34 celebrities, figures of historical importance and assorted other people and objects. What did they all have in common? Yup, all of their names begin with the magical letter 'K'. Kosmic koincidence? No, they all just happened to comprise one particular version of the world according to Kula Shaker.

From Hollywood comedian Danny Kaye to poet John Keats to Frankenstein-monster actor Boris Karloff to former US President John F Kennedy to giant monkey King Kong to hairdresser-defying British funnyman Ken Dodd to a kite – everything and everybody featured on the sleeve apparently played a crucial part in Crispian Mills' daily existence.

Even a kettle.

'Making tea is a very spiritual experience,' explained Kula's lead singer, 'and the kettle is central to that.'

Course it is, mate.

## SMELLS LIKE THIRTEEN SPIRIT

There were 13 tracks on 'K', an extremely lucky choice for an LP that entered the charts at Number One.

Not that the band were immensely impressed by their own crashlanding at pole position.

'It's great, and we all feel like we've achieved something,' said Crispian at the time. 'But then again, Peter Andre got to Number One.'

Back to 'K'. 'Hey Dude' kicked off proceedings in fine, energetic style. 'Knight On The Town' was just as hard'n'heavy, its title a punning reference to Kula's beloved King Arthur and his Knights of the Round Table. 'Temple Of Everlasting Light', with its sitars, tampuras (a four-stringed Indian drone instrument, apparently, like a digeridoo with strings) and tablas, was more Eastern-influenced, a suitable precursor to the next track, 'Govinda'.

More Hammond-battering occurred on 'Smart Dogs', whose melody seemed to be loosely based on 'Pleasant Valley Sunday' by 60s bubblegum rockers, The Monkees. Time for a breather next with 'Magic Theatre', a brief, eerily atmospheric number whose whole lyric consisted of just these lines – 'So I lay my head to rest/All alone it seems/There my guide is waiting/In a world of dreams'.

'Into The Deep' we already knew from the 'Hey Dude' CD single. In fact, if there was one criticism, based on commercial viability rather than aesthetic merit, that could justifiably be levelled at Kula Shaker on this

album, it was that five of the 13 tracks had already been released as singles or as extra tracks on singles.

'Sleeping Jiva' recalled nothing so much as The Doors' apocalyptic Oedipal drama, 'The End'. Then of course there were the hits 'Tattva' and 'Grateful When You're Dead'/'Jerry Was There'.

Next was '303', a tough rocker with an amusing lyric: 'I got my stash/And I love my hash/Think I'll grow myself a big ol' hairy moustache.' Named after the A303 – the rickety expressway to Glastonbury – the song has been described by one enthusiastic journalist as 'possibly the first credible song ever written about being on the road in Britain, capturing the sheer youthful exuberance of hitting the back roads towards the festival with a carload of mates and a boot full of bustables.'

Finally, there was the tuneful simplicity of the Beatlesesque 'Start All Over' and, last but by no means least, the epic 'Hollow Man

(Parts 1 & 2)', the piano-led first part echoing one of the more tranquil interludes on Pink Floyd's 'Dark Side Of The Moon' meisterwerk, the second section building to a monstrously powerful riffing climax, all dense harmonies and layers of guitars.

Individually, the tracks on Kula Shaker's debut album confirmed what their increasing army of acolytes had already suspected: songwriting and ideology aside for a moment, these cats could play.

Kula Shaker's playing was so dexterous, and the four musicians were so steeped in rock history, that they could effortlessly recreate the music of the best rock bands of the last 30 years at will.

Indeed, 'K' could quite easily be re-released and re-marketed by Virgin Records as the next one of their multiple artist compilation albums – say, as 'The Best Trip Pop Album In The World . . . Ever!'

But then again, to their many younger fans, Kula Shaker's knowledge of, and ability

to draw on, all the hundreds and thousands of great rock records of the last three decades were irrelevant.

Simply put, to their teenage audience this was rock'n'roll of a sort they had never heard before, as futuristic to their young ears as Kraftwerk had been to their parents' and The Beatles had been to their grandparents'. Probably.

'It's not retro to me, is it?' an irritated 12-year-old girl at a Kula Shaker gig asked a *Vox* journalist, rhetorically – her question was rhetorical because, of course, the answer, at least to her, was obvious, just as it had been to all those early Beatles fans forced to defend the band against accusations of pilfering the great blues and R&B artists of the 40s and 50s.

### WRITER AT THE GATES OF SCORN

The album 'K' was released to almost unanimous acclaim.

It soon transpired that most of the writers

**Telly shaker**

**The retrospectacular Kula Shaker!**

on the music press, and the reviewers of the CD at the monthly magazines and daily papers – the majority of them men in their late 20s and early 30s – agreed with the 12-year-old girl above: resistance to Kula Shaker's music was not only futile, it was also just about as stupid as lambasting, say, Elvis Presley for being derivative of Bing Crosby.

Not only that, the subtext of their pieces seemed to say, but who ever said that 'new' meant GOOD?

Besides, they argued, it was only Kula Shaker's 'debut', and look how derivative and chock-full of cover versions the debut albums by most innovative and influential rock bands of the past have been.

'"K" is the finest debut you'll hear this year,' acclaimed a jubilant hack from *Vox*. 'It's an audacious record, mixing the retro-rock power of Led Zeppelin, the psychedelic Eastern vibes of George Harrison and the tripped-out balm of The Stone Roses Mk 1.'

'Kula Shaker have swept up on British pop's blind-side with so little help and such unerring force that there is little left for the rest of us to do but gasp in wonder,' opined the gentleman from *The Times*. 'Constructed

and played with enthusiastic brilliance, "K" is one of those rare albums that will become a touchstone for a generation.'

'Musically, they really are good,' decided *Q* magazine. 'They can go from delicacy to harder bluesy riffs and mix harmonies with funky rhythmic undertows to produce a gloriously full sound.'

Day-dreamed style magazine, *iD:* '"K" whirls like a dervish across the pop landscape: picture the scene in *Absolute Beginners* where the mods are out-cooled by acid-tinged dandies and you have a neat metaphor for what Kula Shaker mean today.'

*NME* awarded 'K' a generous nine out of 10: 'An astonishingly confident, musicianly gifted, gloriously hedonistic LP full of the dreamer's poetic optimism.'

Even the Americans, who are generally wary of critically-acclaimed British bands due to the fact that the UK music press tends to welcome new bands like gods, seemingly on a weekly basis, fell for Kula Shaker's debut album.

'Kula Shaker press all the right vintage Britpop buttons on their ripping debut album,' praised *Rolling Stone* magazine, citing all of the band's obvious 60s influences, as well as a few of their more obscure ones, like The Move and The Yardbirds. 'This is a fearlessly derivative retrospectacle of sound and shtick.'

Not that everybody was impressed by the devastating accuracy of Kula Shaker's pop-rock facsimiles.

After considerable exposure to 'K', the writer at *Select* magazine just couldn't seem to get rid of 'the sneaking feeling that you're listening to an obscure 1967 B-side by a band called something like The Lemon Rabbit Hutch,' the magazine's reviewer decided to remain in a blissful state of indecision for his final summing-up line: 'This LP will either turn you into an evangelical neo-hippy or allow endless hours of affectionate amusement.'

However, even the fence-sitters seemed to be able to arrive at but one conclusion: that talent borrows yet genius steals. As the *Independent On Sunday* critic asked: 'Is it

real or is it retro? And does it really matter?'

It did matter to the sole renegade journalist in the pack who had been given the task of reviewing 'K' for the *Melody Maker,* the one writer who just could not get past the fact that, as far as he could hear, every note on Kula Shaker's debut album had already appeared elsewhere before.

'Kula Shaker are so scared of 1996 and want SO BADLY to be dead and reborn in 1972 it's fucking ALARMING,' his words bellowed off the page.

'Crucially,' he added, the bile now rising to his throat, 'retro-accusations are less important than pointing out how deadly dull the bulk of this LP is, in a way that only true scumsucking hippies can be.'

Oh, well. You can't please everybody.

★★★★★★★★★★★★★★★★★★

# Set The Controls For The Heart Of The Fun

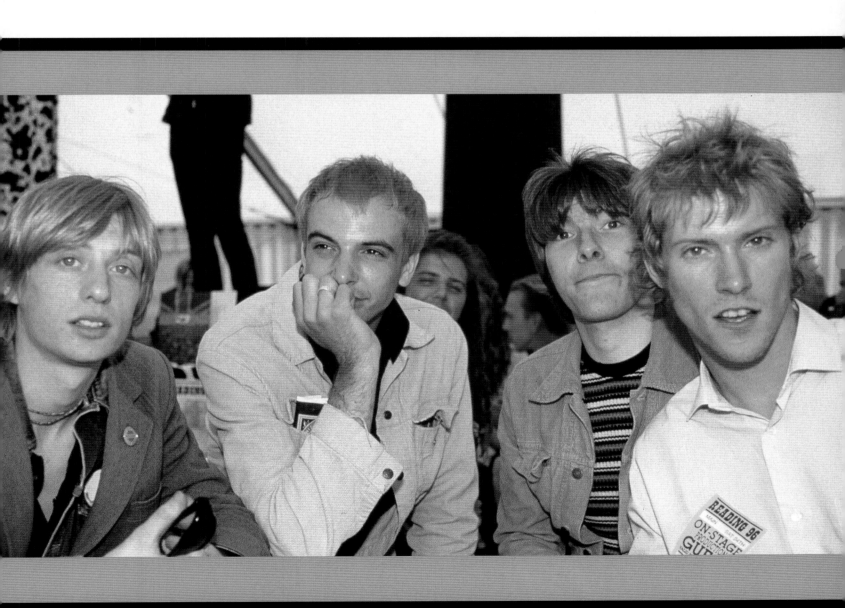

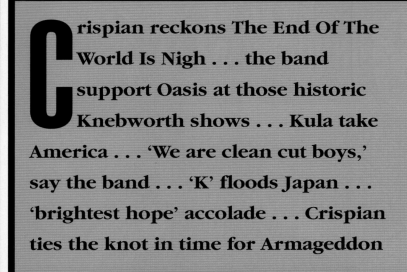

### HIGHER STATE OF CONSCIOUSNESS

Nineteen-ninety-six was the year that witnessed the Death of the Lad and the birth of the New Age Man. Nineteen-ninety-six was the year of Kula Shaker.

'We've worshipped the grail and now our time has come,' stated Crispian Mills, burning with righteously intense self-belief.

'Collectively, our karma has brought us together. Now it's our turn to pass it on through the music, a divine karma for the entire world.

'But,' he added, before he got too carried away, 'we also want to have fun.'

And there you had it: Kula Shaker's comic/serious essence in a nutshell.

'We've got our tongues in our cheeks,' we were assured by these self-styled children of the psychedelic revolution. 'We're having fun and being ironic.'

Not that flippancy was on their agenda. Oh, no. 'It's not about trying to be weird or wacky or sensational,' they said. 'It's about trying to communicate positivity, magic, hope, idealism, adventure and mystery.'

And then, just in case we misunderstood their message, Alonza Bevin warned us once and for all: 'We're not hippies. Hippies stand for apathy, and we're anti-apathy.'

'We certainly don't come from some clichéd hippy thing,' agreed Crispian Mills. 'We're not trying to duplicate anything. We're singing about a NEW era.'

## WE ARE NOT KNEBWORTHY!

In August, Kula Shaker were the chosen supporting act for Oasis at their historic Knebworth shows, which, over two days, drew over 250,000 revellers to a huge field in Hertfordshire.

This, naturally, turned out to be the perfect pre-release advertisement for Kula Shaker and their debut album, 'K'. Listeners were given samples from the album merely one month before it hit the record shops.

succeed where other, more hype-driven bands (for example, Suede), more parochially British bands (say, Blur or Pulp) or more antagonistic and arrogant bands (principally, the fiercely untameable, Yank-insulting Oasis) had failed. 'When I think about breaking America,' Crispian Mills told *Rolling Stone* magazine, 'I think about going there and pressing some social buttons.' He added pointedly: 'I don't think about spitting on TV,' a clear reference to Liam Gallagher

leapt around and shook his blonde mop, *à la* Paul McCartney in his Beatlemaniac days, and the sold-out crowd bobbed vigorously to the Hammond-driven grooves.

At their sell-out show at the 9:30 Club in Washington DC, Kula Shaker whipped the densely packed crowd into a frothing, seething mass: the girls in the audience were squealing at Crispian's cuddly pin-up persona, while the boys in the moshpit were in raptures both at Mills' and Bevin's deft

'Noel has been very good to us,' admitted a well-chuffed Crispian after Kula's outstanding performance, before this tabloid-friendly quote was dragged out of him by an unscrupulous hack: 'Noel Gallagher is nothing like the Oasis projection. But Liam's a bit of a different kettle of fish. I think that boy's got a few problems.'

## AMERICA, THE BEAUTIFUL

Ever since they signed Kula Shaker, Sony had marked them down as one of their Top Priority Acts, with the company's eye on the massive, enormously lucrative American market above all others.

And, as early as the band's first tour of the continent in summer '96, it was quite obvious that Kula Shaker were going to

and his sensationalist dribbling at America's MTV Awards in October.

'If we do crack America, which we will,' a typically confident Mills had said earlier in the year, 'it won't come as any surprise.'

In September, the hardest-working band in showbusiness sold out the prestigious CMJ convention in New York, and then undertook a 10-date tour of the States towards the end of November.

'Those gigs were rocket-fuelled,' Crispian told *Vox.* 'We felt that we played well and everyone was saying, "You guys are awesome."'

At one sold-out show, at The Whiskey in Los Angeles (fittingly, the former haunt of neo-shaman Jim Morrison of The Doors), the band performed terrifically well. Crispian

fretwork, and at the other two, Darlington and Winter-Hart's vicious pummelling of their respective instruments.

Basically, the crowd loved it because, as one breathless young girl gasped backstage after the show, 'We've never really seen or heard anything like this before,' adding unselfconsciously yet revealingly: 'Embarrassingly young, aren't I?'

## SEX'N'DRUGS'N'ROCK'N'. . . MARRIAGE?

Ever since the release of Kula Shaker's single, 'Hey Dude' – a song about the confusion born of excessive hedonism – we were aware that here was a band who were intent on taking a stand against the traditional rock'n'roll creed of instant, selfish gratification of the senses.

How unusual.

That Kula Shaker are not 'rebels', in the narrow rock'n'roll definition of the word, is probably what makes them the most rebellious band around today.

If Kula Shaker stand for anything, the band have claimed, it is individual responsibility, as opposed to freedom of the individual, which Crispian and Co regard as far too bound up with such negative, selfish concepts as nihilism and hedonism.

Talking of which . . . ever since their inception, Kula Shaker have been dramatically committed to 'not using pop music just to sing about sex. We don't believe that you will find freedom by shagging and drinking.'

As Jay Darlington put all this most succinctly: 'We're quite clean, really, for a rock'n'roll band.'

Crispian Mills has spoken at length, and quite graphically, on this very topic.

'It weakens the man if he loses semen all the time,' he once told a journalist. 'So that's why in our culture we have complete unrestricted fucking – anybody, anywhere, as much as we can – and the men have lost their power on a mass scale and the women have gained theirs.'

As if to prove that the band were not in this rock malarkey for the birds and the booze, Crispian Mills got married in '96, simply because, as he explained to an *NME* writer: 'I didn't want to get carried away and lose my sense of reality in this rock star/pop star thing.'

### GIVE 'EM ENOUGH DOPE

Talking of marriage, the other high-profile Britpop star to get hitched in 1996 was John Power of Cast, who also happened to be on Crispian Mills' wavelength *vis-à-vis* consciousness-raising, interstellar visitations, global harmony and the mystical properties of popular music.

And so it was that, under the auspices of *Select* magazine, this recently-founded mutual appreciation society met up (and spliffed up, natch) to discuss everything from fascism to spiritualism to reincarnation

to pyramid power to planetary transformation to the humanitarian crisis to the relative merits of cynicism and idealism in the 1990s.

Hurrah for likeminded pop stars.

## THE FUTURE OF THE WORLD

Of course, Crispian Mills had been discussing the problems facing the planet, and the uncertain future of mankind, all year long, whether or not anybody else was present to support his views or to corroborate his often ludicrous sooth-saying.

'A cataclysmic change is imminent,' Crispian Mills foretold earlier in the year. 'We're on the precipice of something big. We're going to see major changes. I can't wait to be shot down if I'm wrong. But I won't be wrong!'

Crispian may very well be right. After all, he does have lorryloads of astrologists, environmentalists and social scientists who are all on his side.

'Armageddon – it's the planet's destiny,' he railed, warning against the perils of massive-scale environmental abuse. 'That's Mother Nature for you: "Fuck with me," she says, "and I'll fuck right back."'

Crispian Mills had one simple message for mankind in 1996:

The end of the world is nigh.

'It'll be a couple of years, then it'll all start going off in Pakistan, China and India,' he stated with utter assurance, almost as if he had been informed by someone who was in the know. 'The government-funded astrologers in Jaipur, India, are saying that, in 1998, China is going to instigate the Third World War, by uniting the Islamic countries.'

And what exactly will Crispian and the rest of Kula Shaker be doing at this precise moment of thermonuclear meltdown?

'We'll take a ton of rice and a ton of lentils and go underground.'

Kula Shaker are, fairly understandably really, considered by many people to be quite mad.

'I know a lot of people think we're crackpots. But they'll see soon enough that I was right, and that we're not mad.'

And yet all is not lost. Because, at the 11th hour – there is hope!

'If you want to save your life, the world, whatever, just tap into it. It's there.'

Thank God for that.

## THE FUTURE OF KULA SHAKER

Global annihilation or not, Kula Shaker had already pencilled in quite a few things for their next 12 months.

In January 1997, after being voted Brightest Hopes in the weekly music papers, the band went on another successful nationwide tour of Britain.

They were also nominated for the prestigious Brit Award for Best New Band In Britain, and undertook various world jaunts in an attempt to show the rest of the planet what it was missing: in late February, they performed across the States, while in March they made numerous appearances throughout Europe.

As for summer '97, the band have for a long time been tipped to headline one of the main stages at Glastonbury, a long-awaited festival since it had been cancelled the previous June.

Although Kula's first LP, 'K', is still breaking records (it represents, for example, the biggest ever ship-out to Japan of an international act's debut album), their follow-up long-player is expected some time in the autumn.

The band have already started wondering about what the successor to the monster 'K' will be like.

'The next album will hopefully be more spontaneous and earthy,' anticipates Crispian, before going on to ruminate on his own distant future. 'It'd be nice to just chill out a bit. Grow beards. Get dungarees on. Have kids. Get coke habits. You know, the usual things.'

Crispian has always had a warped vision of his own destiny, as he revealed last year.

'I bet when I'm 50 I'm a beggar,' he predicted. 'I'll have nothing. I'll be no use to anybody. No money. The kids'll have gone, if I have any. And it'll be good. I wouldn't mind if I was a beggar, actually.'

Kula prepare for Armageddon

Just before senility kicks in, of course, there lies the little matter of Kula Shaker's number one ambition: that is, naturally, total global domination.

'By the end of the century,' the four have decided, and who would dare to argue, 'we're going to be the biggest band in the world, and to celebrate we're going to play a gig at the Pyramids on the last day of 1999.'

Crispian Mills has absolutely no doubt in his mind just how ginormous this super-gig is going to be. Even if he does keep changing his mind about the location.

'We're going to play a massive gig at Wembley, or somesuch enormodome, and Armageddon will come at a pre-arranged moment,' he said last year, fairly laidback considering the magnitude of his prediction.

'On our final chord,' he continued, the whole affair planned to the minutest detail, 'Armageddon will happen and the spiritual aeroplane from the anti-material world will appear, and we will all climb aboard along with everyone at the concert.

'And then,' he added with a flourish, 'on one last E major 7th chord, we'll all go off to the other side.'

See you there, Crispian.

**Global annihilation, or domination?**